Seasons of Change

Seasons of Change

Understanding Purpose in Times of Perplexity

Myles Munroe

Seasons of Change

Unless otherwise noted, Scripture quotations are taken from the New International Version. Copyright © 1973, 1978, 1984, International Bible Society.

All rights reserved. No portion of this book may be used without written permission of the publisher, with the exception of brief excerpts for magazine articles, reviews, etc.

Copyright © 1998 - Myles Munroe

Printed in the United States of America
ISBN: 1-56229-428-8

Pneuma Life Publishing
4451 Parliament Place
Lanham, MD 20706
(301) 577-4052

Diplomat Press
Dr. Myles Munroe
Diplomat Center
P.O. Box N9583
Nassau, Bahamas
(242) 341-6444

Contents

Dedication
Preface
Introduction

Chapter   Page

1. You Can Be a World Changer! 21
2. The Pursuit of Purpose 25
3. Purpose and the Patriarchs 35
4. The Changing of the Guards 45
5. Mission Fields Becoming Missionaries 59
6. Are You Really Free? 69
7. Look Inside Yourself 77
8. Salvaging the Season 85

Dedication

To the leaders of the past generation whose efforts have provided lessons that inspire and warn us. Thank you for teaching us what to do and sometimes what not to do.

To the leaders of the next generation who have open minds, new methods, and energetic zeal. Dare to be different. May you have the courage to make changes and challenge convention in obedience to the God of all seasons.

To the emerging Third World peoples whose time has come. The quality of the future of your nations, and others, now rests upon you.

To my friends and mentors, Turnel Nelson and Oral Roberts, who have shown me that it is possible to effectively live and contribute to two generations in one lifetime.

Acknowledgments

We are the sum total of all the individuals who have in some way, small or great, contributed to our lives. I learned everything I know from someone. We are all products of what we have gained from others. I thank the multitude of friends, educators, authors, and family members whose lives have contributed to mine.

This work is a synergistic product of these many minds. I am especially grateful to my editors at Pneuma Life Publishing and Mr. Derwin Stewart who encouraged me to complete this work.

A special thanks to my wife Ruth, and children Chrisa and Chairo (Myles, Jr.), who with their patience and support provide the encouragement I need to maximize my season.

Preface

Nothing is as permanent as change. These words transformed my life. Nothing is as constant as change. Change is natural to existence and common to creation. Everything is in a state of change and nothing can stop it. Change is evidence of existence and proof of finiteness. Change is the principle of creation. Everything changes.

This simple statement, *everything changes*, contains a principle that can bring tremendous peace and understanding to life. If we accept the inevitable truth that nothing remains the same and everything will change, it should minimize our level of expectations and disappointments.

In life there are three types of changes: those that happen to us, those that happen around us, and those that we make happen. As there are three types of changes, there are also three types of people in the world: those that watch things, those that make things happen, and those who ask, "what happened?"

There are also generally five types of responses to change: you can resist change, prepare for change, despise or ignore change, accept and adjust to change or initiate and manage change.

One of the greatest tragedies in life is that only a small percentage of the world's population confronts change effectively. Many are victims of change. Some dread change while others refuse to accept it. This is a formula for frustration and depression.

Are you teetering at the threshold of a new season? Perhaps you feel more trepidation than trust right now. You really can learn to embrace change with a positive attitude. As you view transition from God's perspective, you'll find tremendous opportunities for growth. Those new possibilities may hold an exciting destiny for you. Be bold and embrace the next season. It's the only way you'll discover God's purpose for you in this generation.

*"Lost opportunity is the
sacrifice of destiny."*

Introduction

Despite the fact that everything changes, God Himself declares, "I the Lord do not change" (Malachi 3:8). A surface interpretation of this statement may imply that God is stagnant, uncreative, and archaic. But this is far from the truth. In fact, the Scriptures introduce God as Creator, which denotes one who creates and initiates the principle of change. Some have even concluded that as Creator His actions are predicable and His modes of operation unchanging.

To understand this concept of the unchanging nature of God, we must understand the nature of a principle. Principles are principles because they are consistent. The Creator never changes in the sense that, just like a principle, He is consistent. God is always the same in nature, character, and integrity. His acts may change, but His ways never change. *God is predictable in the sense that His nature is consistent and unchanging. He is always one with His supreme self.* His acts and works may vary in type, but they are always consistent with His nature. This understanding is critical to our attitude toward the activities of God in the affairs of men and how this affects our interpretation of the changes in our generation and world.

Change is a component of time. *Time produces change.* Therefore, everything that is within time experiences change. *Time is an interruption in eternity and a measure of forever.* God created time, as recorded in the first book of Moses. Its purpose is clearly stated in the words, ". . . to mark seasons and days and years" (Genesis 1:14). In essence, *time was created to give eternity a measure manifested in seasons and years.* The term seasons denotes change. Therefore, the creation of time became the source of change.

King Solomon stated in his book of wisdom:

There is a time for everything, and a season for every activity under heaven (Ecclesiastes 3:1).

His words capture the spirit of change that is inherent in time. That statement also communicates this principle: *"Everything created below the heavenly, invisible, eternal realm exists in time, and everything in time has a purpose for which there is a season for fulfillment."* In essence, God's purposes and activities in time are designed for seasons, which in turn require change. *Simply put, life in time is lived in seasons and is subject to change. Change is the essence of life in time.*

John Walter, President of AT&T, the world famous telecommunication company, stated, "When the pace of change outside an organization becomes greater than the pace of change inside the organization, the end is near." The principle expressed in this statement is vital for all who wish to maintain effectiveness in a constantly changing world.

Every organization committed to impacting its environment must consider the prospect of change and its ability to respond effectively to that change. No organization exists in a vacuum. Each must submit to the demands of its environment, and the demands vary as the environment changes. Even the most passive organization is compelled in its environment. There are reluctant organizations in aggressive environments.

Organizations, like individuals, should engage in campaigns of self-improvement. Many large organizations have planning departments to ensure a constant stream of innovation. Governments, corporations, military agencies, and other social and civic groups strategize for change. Over the years, however, one organization–the Christian Church–has been criticized for its lack of adaptability. Many believe this criticism is valid. The message and purpose of the Church is constant and unchanging, but its programs, methods, and mechanisms often lag behind the culture and become irrelevant. *The challenge of the church in the 21st century is to adapt without adopting the values of the surrounding culture.* After all, a turn in the road is not the end of the road unless you fail to make the turn.

Throughout history we see the principle of seasons and times in the context of the unfolding of God's providential will.

> There is a time for everything, and a season for every activity under heaven (Ecclesiastes 3:1).

This implies that every aspect of God's purpose is fulfilled within the parameters of times and seasons. Therefore, understanding the principle and nature of times and seasons is critical if we are to properly interpret the activities of God in our generation.

A careful study of history reveals a providential order in the generational progression of mankind. We see evidence of historical convergence and transitional tides at significant points in time. A historical convergence is a strategic period of history when major transitional changes occur, bringing with them drastic and sometimes momentous transformations in social, economic, political, and spiritual conditions. The results of such strategic changes have brought unsettling societal fear, panic, distress, and confusion. Many were not prepared for these changes; others reacted with suspicion, contempt, and violence; while others simply surrendered and became victims of the elements of change.

As we embrace the 21st century, we are also caught in the tides of transitional change. Everyone with a measure of sensitivity, spiritual insight, and historical perspective can sense a historical convergence in every sphere of life. Change is in the air. It is everywhere. The past century brought a tremendous number of history-making events that have undoubtedly shaped the world we live in today.

We can look through the corridor of time at other significant periods in history. Turbulent events belonged to the period known as the dark ages, the age of enlightenment, the age of discovery, the exploits of great explorers such as Christopher Columbus, the expansion of Europe west to the Americas, the slave trade, the colonization era, the birth of the Federal Republic of the United States, World Wars I and II, the creation of the United Nations, the birth of the nation of Israel, the Civil Rights Movement, and the plight of international refugees.

This fascinating century also included great changes in the arena of science, technology, transportation, communication, education, and religion. We've seen the expansion of Islam, the birth and growth of new eastern religions, and the spread of Christianity to the west. The explosion of scientific discoveries led to advances in medicine and the invention of the radio, television, telephone, airplanes, and the computer. The development of inter-continental travel also resulted in intercultural exposures not possible before. The world has been reduced to a global village.

This brief overview of the 20th century graphically captures the complex nature of some of the events that have changed our lives forever. The present transition period demands a response within the context of these changes. What is the nature of the change taking place at this juncture in history? A quick assessment reveals tremendous change in the global political equation. We see the demise of colonialism, the birth and rise of small and large independent states, the extinction of the Cold War, the increase of economic interdependence, and the global access to instant intercultural-international communication through the worldwide web technology and information highway.

Even more significant social and spiritual changes are taking place in the midst of our generation, however. The post World War II leaders are giving way to a generation far removed from that era, bringing a youthfulness to national leadership unseen before now. In the Christian Church, the old guard–Protestant and evangelical leaders and those who fathered the charismatic movement–are drifting from the scene. Their departure makes room for a new crop of leaders for the 21st century church.

A significant shift is taking place in former colonial territories that were once the bastion of mission efforts, many of which are now identified as undeveloped, developing, or Third World countries. The growth of the national church and church leadership in these nations have turned the tables. Former mission fields have now become fields of missionaries. These significant changes demand a new approach and appreciation for effective global missions efforts in this new century.

In this book, we will look at these changes facing the world we must live in and effectively impact with the message of the kingdom of God. We are truly in seasons of change and it will take a well-informed, world-wise, globally-minded, spiritually sensitive, well-trained, purpose-driven army of Christian leaders to effectively make a difference in our generation and set a standard for the generation to come. It will take a leadership which understands the dynamics of change and determines to adjust where necessary. That leadership will have to be creative on demand, and committed to the unchanging gospel of the Lord Jesus Christ—which is the restoration of the kingdom of God on earth. The following pages are intended to provoke you to explore the days of your lifetime and your role and purpose in your generation.

Chapter 1

You Can Be a World Changer!

"Change is evidence of life."

Time and change are inescapable. No matter where you live, no matter what your race or ethnicity, no matter what your language, no matter what your attitude or disposition, eventually time and change will affect you.

Out of all the conditions in the earth, time and change are the most difficult to control. Time ages us, which causes our bodies to grow older and weaker with each passing year. We try to combat the aging process by dyeing our gray hair, wearing false teeth, and applying cosmetics to conceal our wrinkles.

We do these things to preserve ourselves from the effects of time. But–like winter, spring, summer, and fall–time keeps moving.

What does the Bible say about time? Wise King Solomon penned these words, which show how God ordained a time for everything:

> There is a time for everything, and a season for every activity under heaven: a time to be born and a time to die, a time to plant and a time to uproot, a time to kill and a time to hear, a time to tear down and a time to build, a time to weep and a time to laugh, a time to mourn and a time to dance, a time to scatter stones and a time to gather them, a time to embrace and a time to refrain, a time to search and a time to give up, a time to keep and a time to throw away, a time to tear and a time to mend, a time to be silent and a time to speak, a time to love and a time to hate, a time for war and a time for peace (Eccles. 3:1-8).

God also wants us to know there is a time for every type of people. There is a time for the north, and there's a time for the south; there's a time for the outcast, and there's a time for the upper class.

Some have said it's time for change. Change will come whether you prepare for it or not. The wise man uses his time to plan for change. The Bible says the children of Issachar were "men that had understanding of the times, to know what Israel ought to do" (1 Chronicles 12:32, KJV).

How Will You Respond to Change?

Time always produces change in some form. The most inevitable aspect of life is change, and nothing in life is as constant as change. All you can do in relation to change is prepare for it, plan for it, submit to it, manage it, and adjust to it. Time ultimately brings about change, and change always requires a response.

Three types of change constantly confront us:

1. Change that happens around us.

2. Change that happens to us.

3. Change that we make happen.

Since change is inevitable, we should try to ensure that we understand and maximize the benefits of change. Just as there are three types of change, there are also three responses to change.

1. A passive response doesn't react to change.

2. An inquisitive response asks what happened but doesn't try to alter the quality or degree of change.

3. A pro-active response makes things happen.

This third response usually causes change. Pro-active people usually succeed in life—against all odds. I refer to these men and women as "world changers."

Which are you?

It's not what happens to you that matters; it's how you respond to those events. God wants you to prepare for change. Change will happen with or without you, whether you approve or disapprove.

You can become a world changer who makes things happen. How? By discovering your unique, God-given purpose for living and pursuing it with all your might.

> *"When you're through changing, you're through."*

Chapter 2

The Pursuit of Purpose

"Change is a component of purpose"

We are sprinting toward a very strategic point in the relay race of life. The most crucial segment of any relay is the passing of the baton to the next runner. No matter how fast a runner completes his lap, if he fails to pass the baton cleanly, time will be lost. If the runner drops the baton, the race is over.

A track coach may use a stopwatch to time a relay, but is that how God measures our heavenly race? As mortal men and women we use seconds, minutes, hours, days, weeks, months, and years to describe and measure time. But how does God measure your life? The answer may be startling to some.

First, we must understand that God is greater than time and exists outside of it. What is time? The answer is complex yet very simple: *Time is a temporary interruption in eternity.*

If you measure life in terms of years, however, you've got a problem. The Book of Genesis records that some men lived 900 years. That means when they were 200 years old, they were still teenagers. They must have had a long mid-life crisis.

God never intended for us to die. God originally planned for mankind to live forever in a physical body. Eternal life is still God's plan for redeemed man. That's why He's coming back to resurrect our bodies, the last part of born-again man to be redeemed.

This implies that God does not measure life in terms of how long you physically live. So how does God measure the value and success of life? *God measures life in terms of fulfilled purpose!*

Keep Eternity in Your Heart

Scripture declares that God "has also set eternity in the hearts of men" (Ecclesiastes 3:11). God has designed us so that we think in terms of eternity. When one thinks in terms of eternity, he or she must always be aware that time is a temporary element of life.

The God of eternity created time, and He desires us to live our brief lives in time with an eternal perspective. Men become failures and losers when they stop thinking like God.

We are often limited in our service to the Father because we assume it is our personal responsibility to complete a God-given vision in our lifetime. God does not always call one individual to finish the vision that He assigns to a generation.

If you can grasp this, you will avoid being caught up in the stress that is so commonly associated with men and women in ministry. Keep eternity in your heart and you won't get caught in the rush.

You are called to finish your course in the race, but God may give the vision for generations to fulfill. Yours is merely a temporary assignment. Knowing this makes it easy to pass the baton to the next runner. You are not the anchor person in the race but perhaps the first, second, or third leg in the relay. Our anchor is Christ. I have good news for you—He has already finished the race.

Favor is Not Always Length of Life

Many Christians believe that, if you obey the Lord, you will always have a long life. Where did we get that idea? If God measures His favor only in terms of length of life, then Jesus must have disobeyed God because He lived to be only thirty-three and one half years in his physical body as a man. According to Hebrew law a man couldn't actively exercise the office of a priest until he was 30 years of age. In like fashion Jesus' public ministry began only after He turned 30. Therefore, Jesus' earthly ministry lasted only three and a half years.

Most would conclude that is not really long enough to have an effective ministry. By the mere fact of our born again experience, however, we know that Jesus' ministry was effective. Why? Because He fulfilled the two unequivocal purposes for which He came to earth. As the Son of Man, Jesus destroyed the works of Satan by overcoming the works of sin in the flesh.

> He that committeth sin is of the devil; for the devil sinneth from the beginning. For this purpose the Son of God was manifested, that he might destroy the works of the devil (1 John 3:8, KJV).

As the Son of God, Jesus Christ redeemed man from sin, reconciling us back to God and bringing salvation to the world so that the kingdom of God could be restored to man. When Jesus finished those two tasks, He cried out from the cross, "It is finished!" and yielded up His spirit. Through His resurrection Jesus further conquered the last enemy of man–death!

Length of life is related to purpose. Have you heard this statement: "Only the good die young"? In my opinion, people such as John F. Kennedy and Martin Luther King, Jr. died young because they fulfilled their purpose. It does seem that the good die young, but they also die when their purpose is complete. You live until you finish the purpose He sent you to earth to fulfill.

God always gives time for purpose to be fulfilled. If the purpose for which you have been born needs 50 more years to be accomplished, God will keep you alive. If your assigned purpose takes only 25 years to fulfill, you will have 25 years. If you need to live until age 90 to complete God's purpose for your life, He will keep you alive 90 years. When you finish your God-given assignment, you will leave this life. However, the key is you must discover and commit yourself to the completion of that purpose.

Have you ever wondered why many wicked people live so long? God will keep a man alive and hope that he finds his purpose. Never pray for a wicked man to die because one day he might become one of the greatest leaders in your nations.

What is Purpose?

God measures life in terms of purpose. Therefore, everything and everyone has a God-ordained purpose. But what is purpose? It's the original intent or the reason for the existence of a thing.

Purpose is in the mind of the manufacturer. The only one who knows the original intent for a particular thing is the one who created it. If you don't know the reason something exists, there's only one thing you can do with it–abuse it! The word *abuse* comes from two words, *abnormal use*.

The only way to use something in its normal, correct state and for optimal performance is to discover the purpose for which it was created. Consequently, if you don't know the purpose of a particular thing, you will inevitably abuse it and it may eventually destroy you. This includes your own life.

The apostle Paul's first letter to the Corinthians had an important purpose: to address the abuse of the gifts (graces) of the Holy Spirit. The church at Corinth was abusing (abnormally using) the gifts of the Spirit for personal edification and gratification. Therefore, this epistle carried a corrective element. Paul explained they didn't know how to correctly use the gifts of the Spirit because they were ignorant of the gifts' purpose. Because they were carnal and childish, Paul was unable to communicate with them on an adult level.

Children are ignorant of the purposes of complex things. If you give a child a chainsaw, he will probably harm himself and others. Why? Because the child is ignorant of the saw's purpose; he doesn't know how to use it correctly. For that reason any responsible adult would withhold it from him.

Conversely, the apostle Paul's letter to the Galatian church was for the purpose of imparting to them the reality of their liberty in Christ. Legalistic Judaizers had attempted to impose upon the Galatian Christians the requirements and demands of the Law. Paul explicitly told them that they were not justified by their adherence to the Law but by their faith in Jesus Christ. He admonished them not to frustrate the grace of God by trying to seek righteousness through the Law.

Paul concluded his admonishment to the Galatians with this encouragement:

> Stand fast therefore in the liberty wherewith Christ hath made us free, and be not entangled again with the yoke of bondage.... Christ is become of no effect unto you, whosoever of you are justified by the law; ye are fallen from grace. For we through the Spirit wait for the hope of righteousness by faith.... For, brethren, ye have been called unto liberty; only use not liberty for an occasion to the flesh, but by love serve one another (Galatians 5:1,4,5,13, KJV).

You must see that everything and everyone has a purpose.

Paul's letter to the Corinthian church imposed ordinances and regulations necessary for the godly, correct functioning of that church. Unlike his epistle to the Corinthians, Paul's letter to the Galatians lifted the regulations and bondages imposed upon them by the Law.

The apostle Paul reminds us that God is a God of purpose:

> That in the dispensation of the fulness of times he [God] might gather together in one all things in Christ, both which are in heaven, and which are on earth; even in him: in whom also we have obtained an inheritance, being predestined according to the purpose of him who worketh all things after the counsel of his own will (Ephesians 1:10,11, KJV).

Everything God does with us, for us, to us, and through us is to accomplish His purpose on the earth. *We are saved by God for a purpose, ordained by God for a purpose, appointed of God for a purpose, and anointed of God for a purpose—His purpose.*

If you, as a man or woman, want to know how to run a good race and finish the course that God has specifically assigned to you, you must find and pursue the God-ordained purpose for your life. Your unique purpose will find its expression in and through the Body of Christ.

What is God's purpose for the Church? It's not a social gathering place; it's not an organization that merely builds buildings; it's not a vehicle for entertainment; neither is it a nursery for Christian babies who refuse to grow up. God intends the Church to be so glorious and mighty in the earth that it would display God's wisdom to angels and demons alike.

> His intent was that now, through the church, the manifold wisdom of God should be made known to the rulers and authorities in the heavenly realms, *according to his eternal purpose* which he accomplished in Christ Jesus our Lord (Ephesians 3:10,11).

The Church is Heaven's earthly agency–designed to train it's members to fulfill their purpose on earth in their generation.

You can be involved in God's exciting plan for this generation. Begin to shift your focus from the temporal things of this life to the eternal purposes of the kingdom of God. Endeavor to know God, to seek first His kingdom, and to invest your life in people.

> *"The fact that you were born is evidence that there is a purpose you must fulfill."*

Chapter 3

Purpose and the Patriarchs

*"To everything a season...
every purpose a time."*

God has been using imperfect men and women to accomplish His perfect will for thousands of years. God may have emphasized different aspects of His agenda in each age, but His overall plan was established.

Let's look at God's purpose and how the patriarchs handed it down from generation to generation. They all understood the principle of purpose, seasons, and time and successfully transferred the baton from generation to generation.

Abraham, the great patriarch of the Israelite nation, was chosen by God for one specific purpose: to father Isaac, the promised child who would be the progenitor of God's chosen nation, Israel. God chose **Jacob,** like his grandfather Abraham, for the purpose of planting biological seed that inevitably would bring about the twelve tribes of Israel. **Joseph,** the favored son of Jacob, was assigned the purpose of governing the agricultural storehouses of Egypt, the land destined to be the Israelites' place of captivity for 400 years. His purpose was to preserve the chosen nation until the deliverance.

Moses was chosen by God to fulfill two specific purposes in his lifetime. First, Moses delivered the people of Israel out of Egyptian captivity. Second, Moses declared the Law of God to Israel and God's will for them as a nation. God desired Israel to be a nation of priests—God's representatives and witnesses to the world of His goodness, greatness, and desire to reconcile fallen man back to Himself. Even though Moses was an orphan, a murderer, and a fugitive, God still used him to fulfill His purpose among the Israelites.

God always works everything with purpose. God sets your life from birth for a purpose. According to the plan of Pharaoh, Moses was destined to die as an infant. God had different plans for Moses, however, and His plan prevailed.

> Many are the plans in a man's heart, but it is the Lord's purpose that prevails (Proverbs 19:21).

Can You See Success?

After the death of Moses, God's agenda continued in the life of **Joshua**. He settled the children of Israel in the land that God had promised to the patriarch Abraham over 400 years earlier.

Forty years before the Israelites entered the promised land, Moses sent Joshua and 11 other leaders from the 12 tribes of Israel into Canaan to spy out the land. Moses gave them these specific instructions:

> See what the land is like and whether the people who live there are strong or weak, few or many. What kind of land do they live in? Is it good or bad? What kind of towns do they live in? Are they unwalled or fortified? How is the soil? Is it fertile or poor? Are there trees on it or not? Do your best to bring back some of the fruit of the land (Numbers 13:18-20).

Upon their return, 10 of the 12 spies brought back an evil or negative report.

> We went into the land to which you sent us, and it does flow with milk and honey! Here is its fruit. But the people who live there are powerful, and the cities are fortified and very large (Numbers 13:27,28).

The two young Army Captains, Caleb and Joshua, however, saw something entirely different. Even though there were giants in the land,

Caleb said,

> Let us go up at once, and possess it; for we are well able to overcome it (Numbers 13:30, KJV).

One characteristic of those who possess a keen sense of their God-ordained purpose is their ability to exercise spiritual vision. *People of purpose are people of vision.* Purpose gives you the ability to see success even in the face of seemingly insurmountable obstacles. People of purpose possess spiritual wisdom along with divine vision.

Out of that entire generation which had seen God's miracles in Egypt and the wilderness, only Joshua and Caleb entered the promised land. Their vision of success enabled them to experience the goodness of Canaan.

Don't Neglect Your Purpose!

David, a man of war, defeated all the enemies of Israel so the nation could live in peace. His purpose was to establish peace for the nation in order to create an environment for the construction of a permanent house for God to dwell among men. He expanded the borders of Israel and made Jerusalem its religious and political capital. He manifested the earthly prototype of what the Messiah, Jesus, would be to God's chosen people, Israel. David foreshadowed the ideal model kingship that eventually would be fulfilled in Jesus

Christ, the King of kings and Lord of lords. Born of David's family line, Jesus will ultimately rule and reign over God's never-ending kingdom.

David failed in life only when he neglected to pursue his God-ordained purpose. One spring, when kings usually went forth to battle, David stayed at Jerusalem. He sent Joab and the Israelite army to destroy the Ammonites and besiege Rabbah.

> One evening David got up from his bed and walked around on the roof of the palace. From the roof he saw a woman bathing. The woman was very beautiful, and David sent someone to find out about her. The man said, "Isn't this Bathsheba, the daughter of Eliam and the wife of Uriah the Hittite?" Then David sent messengers to get her. She came to him, and he slept with her.... Then she went back home. The woman conceived and sent word to David, saying, "I am pregnant" (2 Samuel 11:2-5).

When David neglected his purpose–fighting the enemies of Israel–he became susceptible to the temptations of lust and fell into sin.

David's moral failure shows us several things we must understand if we want to successfully accomplish the purpose of God for our lives.

First, irresponsibility produces boredom. If it is not replaced with responsible activity, boredom inevitably results in sin.

Second, sin is a distraction from the plan, purpose, and will of God for your life.

Third, sin's consequences bring death to the purposes of God for your life as well as death to your spirit and body. God forgives sin, but the wages of sin–even to the believer–is still death. Most of the time sin brings death to relationships, whether it's our relationship with God, family, or friends.

Sin, without exception, produces death.

The only solution to death is God's resurrection as expressed through His Holy Spirit. David's sin caused the death of the child he conceived with Bathsheba; death in his relationships with his children; the actual death of two more of his children; and separation in his relationship with God.

What's the moral of this story? If you want to avoid failure, become so busy fulfilling your purpose that you don't have time to sin.

Be Wholehearted Toward God

Solomon had one specific purpose in life: to build the house of the Lord. God instilled in him an amazing ability for administration and commerce. Whatever your purpose, you can be assured that God has instilled in you, even from birth, the abilities, talents, and gifts necessary to successfully carry out the particular assignments ascribed to your purpose.

The abuse of God-given talents and gifts, however, can lead to an aberration of purpose and a retardation of personal character. Solomon's abuse of his ability to network the talents, influence, and resources of others caused him to enter unholy alliances with foreigners. Like Adam and Abraham, Solomon allowed the women in his life to cause him to disobey the commandment of God. The Bible declares that, when Solomon was old, "his wives turned his heart after other gods, and his heart was not fully devoted to the Lord his God, as the heart of David his father had been" (1 Kings 11:4).

Solomon in all his glory and accomplishments still speaks as one who did not heed the word of the Lord to his fathers:

> Be careful that you do not forget the Lord your God, failing to observe his commands, his laws and his decrees that I am giving you this day. Otherwise, when you eat and are satisfied, when you build fine houses and settle down, and when your herds and flocks grow large and your silver and gold increase and all you have is multiplied, then your heart will become proud and you will forget the Lord your God, who brought you out of Egypt, out of the land of slavery (Deuteronomy 8:11-14).

What is God's purpose for wealth? God wants His covenant established and His kingdom furthered. Don't let wealth divert you from the purposes of God.

You Have Everything You Need

When God called Moses to fulfill his purpose, he was an expert manager who had been trained in Pharaoh's court. God refined his character for 40 years as he led sheep in the wilderness. He became an excellent shepherd.

One day God said, "Moses, I know you can handle the responsibility that awaits you. I'll take away the sheep and give you three million people."

God always makes demands on you based on the potential He has given you. Whatever your purpose, your potential is equal to the task. Your potential springs from the source that created you.

God is all-powerful or omnipotent. Omni means "all." Potent means "ability un-manifested." Therefore, God has everything you have not seen yet. All things that exist have no more potential than the source from which they came. A wooden table is only as strong as its wood.

Whatever God desires, He decides what He wants it made from, and then He speaks it into existence. When God wanted us, He spoke to Himself.

> Let us make man in our image, in our likeness (Genesis 1:26).

Whatever your purpose, God has already given you the potential to fulfill it. Whatever God calls for, He provides for. When He gives vision, He gives the provision necessary to accomplish it. Therefore, your potential is not determined by you but by the demands made upon it by the One Who created you. *Ability is determined by demand.*

If God has called you to do a particular thing, consider it done. Whatever God asks you to do, in His prophetic sight it is already complete. Therefore it's too late to give an excuse. It doesn't matter what anyone says. The only thing that matters is what God wants of your life.

Wherever something originates, it has to stay attached to it's source in order to survive. Plants spring from the earth. They have to stay attached to the ground in order to live. Mankind came from God, and we've got to abide in Him in order to live.

Sin is declaration of independence from your source. That is why sin separates us from the presence of God. Just as a plant can't live without soil, you can't live without God.

If you want to be successful in fulfilling your purpose in life, you must maintain a continual communion with your heavenly Father. Why? Out of Him comes everything necessary to live with purpose and meaning.

> For in him we live and move and have our being (Acts 17:28).

Why is it so important to abide in Christ at this time? God is bringing great change to the Body of Christ. As He shakes whatever can be shaken, we must stay close to God, listen for His voice, and get ready for the next move of His Spirit.

"It's never too late to change."

Chapter 4

The Changing of the Guards

"The initiation and management of change is the ultimate test of leadership."

When the Bible refers to a guard, it usually uses the word "watchman." A watchman is a military guard or commander who stands on a fortress and watches over walled cities. God calls spiritual leaders in the Body of Christ to watch over His people, guarding the citizens of the kingdom from external and internal enemies.

The presence of a watchman implies something needs to be protected. You post a guard when an adversary tries to steal or harm something that you value. Although guards may appear in full military dress, they are not models who merely display their uniforms. Guards usually carry weapons to protect what is being guarded. That implies the possibility of impending conflict.

The presence of a guard implies three things:

1. Something is in danger of being harmed by an adversary.
2. Something is worth being protected.
3. Something is of such great value that the guard risks his life to defend it.

If God has called you to leadership in His Body, the first issue you must consider is not how well you're going to live but how willing you are to die. Are you willing to die to your opinions, your rights, your will, and your way? Ultimately, you may even have to give up life itself to remain true to Christ.

Many people enter the ministry because they're enticed by the glamour and the trappings of wealth that can afford them a better life. If you aren't willing to sacrifice your personal comfort, however, you shouldn't be involved in any type of ministry. If you don't possess the conviction for Him that is worth dying for, you don't deserve the benefits that are worth living for.

Do We Know Our Enemy?

Who is the adversary? It's not any particular church or denomination; it's not the seminary or some religious institution; it's not your brother or sister in the Lord; nor is the adversary the governmental or political leaders of the day.

Our adversary may use these people and institutions as instruments to accomplish his purposes. The adversary, however, has been clearly identified in the Word of God:

> For though we walk in the flesh [in human bodies] we do not war after the flesh [using mere human weapons] (2 Corinthians 10:3, KJV).

> For we wrestle not against flesh and blood [human beings], but against principalities, against powers, against the rulers of darkness of this world, against spiritual wickedness in high places [demonic beings and forces] (Ephesians 6:12, KJV).

Knowing that we are engaged in battle with demonic beings, we must rely on the supernatural ability of the living Word of God and the power of the Holy Spirit to combat such forces. Scripture declares:

> (For the weapons of our warfare are not carnal [fleshly], but mighty through God to the pulling down of strong holds;) casting down imaginations, and every high thing that exalteth itself against the knowledge of God, and bringing into captivity every thought to the obedience of Christ (2 Corinthians 10:4,5, KJV).

Imaginations refer to our thought process, and strongholds are solidified ways of thinking that result from our exposure to and acceptance of demonic influence. Whether our marred thinking results from some ideology—or some perverted image from television, pornography, or violence—the source is ultimately demonic. Our wrong thinking may even result from erroneous theology or religious tradition. It makes no difference to the enemy of your soul. Satan wants to deceive you, rob you of abundant life, and destroy you.

Looking at 2 Corinthians 10:3-5 in its context, we can conclude that the devil primarily assaults our minds. Why does he target this battlefield? If Satan controls our thoughts and the manner in which we think, he can cause us to doubt the validity, effectiveness, and truthfulness of God's life-changing Word. Therefore, we must guard the spirit of our mind with all diligence. We are to gird up the loins of our minds with the uncompromising truth—God's eternal, unadulterated Word.

What Do We Protect?

As guards and watchmen on the wall, what are we responsible for protecting? First, we are not called to protect the gospel; neither are we called to protect the Lord Jesus Christ. The devil has already tried to kill Christ, and Christ has prevailed over the enemy by rising from the dead.

We definitely don't have to protect God. He's the All-Sufficient One. As watchmen, we are not called to protect man's agenda, personal beliefs, or denominational boundaries.

So what are we called to protect?

We must guard our faith in God and the redeeming work of the Lord Jesus Christ in our lives. Finally, we must protect God's vision for our lives, families, ministries, and churches. We must examine the sphere of influence that God has entrusted to us and make certain that our every decision coincides with that vision.

What's Worth Dying For?

The traditions of men, regardless of how sacred you may think they are or how long they have been in effect, are not worth dying for. Generally, tradition means the passing down of elements of a culture from generation to generation or a body of unwritten religious precepts.

We must protect our purpose for life, not our traditions. Traditions may change but purpose is permanent.

The English word *tradition* comes from the same Latin word that denotes trade and transaction.

Trade implies an item that has been patterned. That's why you can trade it. Whenever an individual or business develops a trade, they have patterned something that they wish to export to other persons or businesses. Our churches and denominations have done the same thing with our traditions.

When many Western missionaries brought the gospel to Africa, South America, Latin America, the Far East, and the Caribbean islands, they exported Western culture and idealism with it. A great deal of that culture was and still is contrary to the authentic representation of the Christianity—and the Christ—of the Bible.

All cultures, religious systems, and denominations have something that's good and worth trading. We must be led of the Holy Spirit and rooted in the prudent interpretation of God's Word, however, as we judge those things. We must be careful how we trade.

Traditions that are effective and consistent with the Word of God are fine. When our traditions lose their beneficial nature, however, we should discard them.

Jesus told the Pharisees and scribes that they emasculated the Word of God by the insistent keeping of their traditions.

Thus have ye made the commandment of God of none effect by your tradition (Matthew 15:6, KJV).

Your tradition is not worth dying for, only the Truth of God's Word.

Finally, we must be cautious in protecting what we call our theology, understanding that our beliefs and convictions are grounded in biblical truth. Truth is not relative but progressive. Your theological beliefs are almost certain to change as you mature in the Lord and become more exercised in the Word of God. The writer of Hebrews expected these believers to progress in their knowledge of God:

Anyone who lives on milk, being still an infant, is not acquainted with the teaching about righteousness. But solid food is for the mature, who by constant use have trained themselves to distinguish good from evil (Hebrews 5:13,14).

You probably believe some things now that you didn't believe five years ago. Likewise, you probably discarded some beliefs that you held five years ago. You may have been very dogmatic about those beliefs, insisting that the Holy Spirit told you those things. In actuality, those beliefs were probably your *opinions* of God's Word based on your spiritual growth and conviction at the time.

Because of a limited perspective of the Word of God, your opinions may have been deficient. We must be very careful when we say, "Thus saith the Lord," because it may very well be, "Thus saith my opinion." The apostle Paul said:

> For we know in part, and we prophesy in part. But when that which is perfect is come, then that which is in part shall be done away. When I was a child, I spake as a child, I understood as a child, I thought as a child: but when I became a man, I put away childish things. For now we see through a glass, darkly; but then face to face: now I know in part; but then shall I know even as also I am known (1 Corinthians 13:9-12, KJV).

When he was a child, the apostle Paul didn't think maturely. Our incorrect assessment of right and wrong often results from our limited experience, exposure, knowledge, and counsel from the Spirit of God. Paul was an apostle who had received such revelation from God that it was unlawful for him to speak all the things he knew, yet he declared to the church at Corinth that even "now I know in part..."

On another occasion Paul wrote that even in the face of all of his vast knowledge, wisdom, and revelation from God, he still did not count himself as one who had apprehended in fullness the things of God.

Not that I have already obtained all this, or have already been made perfect, but I press on to take hold of that for which Christ Jesus took hold of me (Philippians 3:12).

Because all of us, young and old alike, should be growing spiritually (being transformed from glory to glory), our theologies at different times are always somewhat unstable and continually metamorphosing into the knowledge of God. Therefore your theological opinions are not worth dying for.

So what is worth dying for?

According to the Word of God, the only thing worth dying for is your faith in Jesus Christ. We believe that Jesus is the Christ, the only begotten Son of God the Father Who died for our sins, arose from the dead to live forever, and is now seated at the right hand of God Almighty. That and that alone is worth dying for.

The apostle Paul told Timothy, "Fight the good fight of faith" (1 Timothy 6:12, KJV), or contend (battle) for the faith. Until your faith is worth dying for, it isn't worth living for. It is this unmovable faith that binds us to our purpose in life and gives us the impetus to adapt to God's seasons of change.

Why a Change?

When talking about the changing of the guards, five fundamental questions come to mind.

Who is changing the guards? God is sovereignly orchestrating this transition among His people. It's not the result of some conference mandate or denominational decree. It's not the innovation of some particular group of men and women. The restructuring of traditional church order, the changing of evangelistic and ministerial methodology, and the raising up of visionary, progressive leaders in the Body of Christ results from God refashioning His Church for 21st century evangelism and ministry.

God changes things in the Church and the world without anyone's permission. Almighty God is both omnipotent and omniscient. Therefore, those who seek to oppose this great awakening must be careful lest they be found fighting against the will of God.

What will replace the old guards? Let's look at the difference in leadership that existed among the 12 tribes of Israel during their 40 years of wandering through the wilderness. All 12 spies saw the same thing as they traveled throughout Canaan, but Caleb and Joshua came back with a different report. Why? These two leaders viewed life from a different perspective.

Unlike the others, Caleb and Joshua were not overwhelmed by the challenges that lay before them. They were confident God would help them overcome even what appeared to be insurmountable circumstances. They were more convinced of the promise of God to their forefathers than they were dismayed by the difficulties before them.

This is precisely the type of leadership God is raising up in this hour. These men and women of courage have the audacity to believe God even in the midst of seemingly impossible situations. These leaders are convinced that "with man this is impossible, but with God all things are possible" (Matthew 19:26).

What distinguishes these guards from previous ones? *Their courage will be tempered with character; their determination will be disciplined by wisdom; their victories will be achieved through God-inspired vision; and their God-given promises will be governed by God-ordained purpose.*

These men and women are not seeking the promises of God for personal prosperity; instead, they seek God for the prosperity that will enable them to convert their communities and their cultures to Christ. These men and women are not motivated by greed. They understand that the grace of God is given to further His kingdom and not their own personal agendas. These are the kind of men and women that God is calling to the forefront of this great move of God. These leaders don't care who gets the credit, they are committed to completing the work

When will God change the guards? God is doing it right now. The spiritually astute among us know that the transitions in government, widespread natural disasters and tragedies, and the instability in religious denominations indicate that God is changing things drastically. The changing of the guards is upon us. We must submit and enthusiastically embrace what the God of all creation is doing.

Where is this awakening taking place? This great and mighty move of God is taking place all over the world, especially in Third World nations. Africa and the Caribbean nations are set ablaze with revival and evangelistic fires. Out of these nations God is raising up mighty men and women of God whose tongues are set afire with the truth of God's Word. Their minds have been sharpened with sound, biblical, missions-oriented theology; their hearts purified with godly character; and their spirits filled with the power of God's Holy Spirit.

Why do we need to change the guards? Change becomes necessary when a methodology is no longer effective. *The American Heritage Dictionary* defines obsolete as "outmoded in design, style, or construction.... Increasingly vestigial or disappearing in each succeeding generation."

Many, although not all, the leaders who presently govern the affairs of churches and ministries are no longer effective in transforming this present generation. Many attempt to pour new wine into old wine skins, and it just won't work. We are trying to win 1990s gang bangers and drug lords with a 1980s church boy methodology and approach to ministry. Like the Pharisees and scribes who held onto their traditions, we lack the power and wisdom to win a generation who are without God-given purpose and vision.

Many Christians may call themselves leaders, but they are nothing more than managers who feebly maintain the status quo. As I travel the world I am amazed at the number of Christian leaders who are utterly out of touch with the world that God has called them to impact.

Why must we prepare for change? Many present day leaders lack the ability to relate to their constituency. Our society now enjoys global telecommunications, enabling us to use new vehicles to reach the masses for Christ. *We need assertive, visionary leaders with pure motives and godly ambition to take us to the next level of transforming our societies and cultures with the gospel.* All these signs indicate a great necessity for change in Christian leadership and kingdom representation.

There is clearly a kingdom mandate for the changing of the guards.

"Not all change is improvement, but without change there can be no improvement."

Chapter 5

Mission Fields Becoming Missionaries

"You will only become what you are becoming right now."

One aspect of this awakening challenges former mission fields, primarily in the Third World, to become missionaries throughout the developed world. Before we can realize our potential to impact other nations, however, we must examine our past.

We are products of history. We don't want to be chained to our past, but we must understand it to appreciate the present. With all the challenges that face us, we must gain a God-inspired vision of our glorious future–not just in Heaven but in this life.

God's Purpose for Slavery

At the turn of the century, western Europe developed inventions and organizations that enabled them to gradually control others and thereby acquire great wealth. They began to search for new worlds to conquer. North and South America were both rich and easy to control. Asia was rich but difficult to control. Africa was poor and scarcely worth controlling.

When the colonial powers spread over the world, they entered different nations that already had their own culture. They came to a land, settled in the place, made it their own, and used the land for their benefit. For example, Europe benefited from the tropical areas that produced tobacco, sugar, and cotton.

As the European powers exerted their influence over the world, many African people were captured, placed on ships, and sold into slavery in faraway lands. As deplorable as slavery was, God still used it for His purposes. Read what the apostle Paul said to an audience at Athens:

> From one man he [God] made every nation of men, that they should inhabit the whole earth; and he determined the times set for them and the exact places where they should live. God did this so that men would seek him and perhaps reach out for him

and find him, though he is not far from each one of us (Acts 17:26,27).

The Bible says God decides where people will live. God determines where nations will be formed. God also prophesied this to Isaiah:

> This is what the Lord says: "The products of Egypt and the merchandise of Cush [the dark-skinned race], and those tall Sabeans–they will come to you and will be yours; they will trudge behind you, coming over to you in chains. They will bow down before you and plead with you, saying, 'Surely God is with you, and there is no other; there is no other god'" (Isaiah 45:14).

Cush is the word for black man. You may have thought the British or Dutch instituted slavery of dark-skinned people, but God *permitted* this to happen.

Why did God relocate many of our ancestors? The purpose was transportation not slavery. The Bible says that God creates nations for His purpose so that men might know Him.

The United States began as one nation under God. That was God's purpose. Whenever people forget their purpose, they destroy themselves. The minute you move away from your purpose for existing, you begin to self-destruct.

The prosperity and purpose of the industrial States and Europe was to share the gospel and to equip the undeveloped nations to do the same. The nations that subjected and oppressed the undeveloped peoples also sent their great great-grandchildren to tell them about God.

No matter what your ethnic heritage, you are today where your purpose demanded. God determined for you to live somewhere for a purpose. Wherever you're planted, grow. Don't complain, just grow. Find your purpose and move with it into the future. Don't focus on the past because you can't change the past. There is a time and season for every purpose.

When the seasons change, you've got to recognize the signs and make the necessary transition. Each season brings unique opportunities that we must seize. Solomon contrasted two men who approached seasons differently. The same principle applies to spiritual matters:

> He who gathers crops in summer is a wise son, but he who sleeps during harvest is a disgraceful son (Proverbs 10:5).

I thank God for the missionaries who brought us His Word. We who were once mission fields, however, have come to the crossroads. The season has changed. Now God wants us to impact other nations with the gospel and not merely be impacted by European or Western missionaries.

Why Remain a Mission Field?

Unfortunately, it is easier for Third World nations to remain mission fields. Why? Because a mission field is only concerned with receiving from others. If you keep on receiving, you'll never become a blessing to someone who needs you to invest in them.

Some missionaries didn't want our nations to become self-sufficient because our lack benefited their cause. They wanted to keep us poor so they could take pictures, return to their churches, and raise more money for our poverty-stricken land.

Unfortunately, they didn't realize one important truth: Success without a successor is actually failure. If missionaries leave without raising up local persons to carry on the work, they have failed.

The responsibility for success or failure also falls on the shoulders of those in whom missionaries have invested. People don't want to become missionaries because they don't want to grow up and take responsibility. These people prefer staying mission fields.

"If Only We Had Died!"

Look at the Israelites, who were enslaved by the Egyptians for generations. Oppressed by cruel taskmasters, the Israelites lifted their hands and prayed, "Set us free from all our troubles, Lord." They cried to God for 400 years.

One day the Lord called Moses and appointed him to release His people from bondage. After God struck the land with a series of plagues, Moses led the Israelites out of Egypt and into the desert where they were totally dependent on God.

After camping near the waters of Elim, the Israelites set out on the fifteenth day of the second month of their freedom from Egyptian bondage. They soon found themselves in the Desert of Sin.

> In the desert the whole community grumbled against Moses and Aaron. The Israelites said to them, "If only we had died by the Lord's hand in Egypt! There we sat around pots of meat and ate all the food we wanted, but you have brought us out into this desert to starve this entire assembly to death" (Exodus 16:2,3).

The people complained, "Moses, you have forced us to grow up! Why did you do that?" The Israelites prayed for freedom for 400 years and when it happened, they wished they had died in slavery.

Like many of us, the Israelites quickly grumbled when faced with adversity. Some people don't like independence because independence costs too much. People who have been in bondage also fear when responsibility arrives.

God, however, wanted the entire nation to trust Him totally. Seeing their need for sustenance, God miraculously provided manna from Heaven, quail, and water from a rock. However the Israelites continued to doubt God's goodness, power, and provision.

"Let's Go Back to Egypt!"

After sending 12 spies throughout Canaan, Moses heard a bad report that disheartened the people. The Israelites rebelled against entering the promised land and actually made plans to return to Egypt.

> That night all the people of the community raised their voices and wept aloud. All the Israelites grumbled against Moses and Aaron, and the whole assembly said to them, "If only we had died in Egypt! Or in this desert! Why is the Lord bringing us to this land only to let us fall by the sword? Our wives and children will be taken as plunder. Wouldn't it be better for us to go back to Egypt?" And they said to each other, "We should choose a leader and go back to Egypt" (Numbers 14:1-4).

When Moses and Aaron heard this, they fell on their faces before the assembly. Joshua and Caleb, who had spied out the land and returned with a good report, tore their clothes and exhorted the people with these words:

> The land we passed through and explored is exceedingly good. If the Lord is pleased with us, he will lead us into that land, a land flowing with milk and honey, and will give it to us. Only do not rebel against the Lord. And do not be afraid of the people of the land, because we will swallow them up. Their protection is gone, but the Lord is with us. Do not be afraid of them (Numbers 14:7-9).

What can we learn from this example? If we don't go into that land—and take responsibility for our season now—our children are going to suffer for our inactivity and lack of faith. If we don't become missionaries now, then our great-grandchildren will be four generations behind.

God forgives our irresponsibility, but sin still has consequences. When Moses asked God not to destroy the entire nation in His anger, He replied:

> I have forgiven them, as you asked. Nevertheless... not one of the men who saw my glory and the miraculous signs I performed in Egypt and in the desert but who disobeyed me and tested me ten times—not one of them will ever see the land I promised on oath to their forefathers. No one who has treated me with contempt will ever see it (Numbers 14:20,23).

People in general, like the Israelites, fear responsibility. If we don't shoulder responsibility, we remain the same. If we remain the same, we give no hope to ourselves or the next generation.

What can we conclude about those who shrink back from the challenge of becoming missionaries who have a vision to impact others? What happens if you remain a mission field:

1. You don't have to lead. You'll always be led.

2. You don't need to make decisions. They will be made for you.

3. You don't have to provide for yourself or others. Your needs will be met.

4. You'll become attached to traditions, which are designed to stop you from thinking.

5. Your irresponsibility has serious consequences—for yourself and others.

God has called former mission fields to become missionaries, but are these people more concerned with receiving or giving? A self-centered approach to life may be satisfying for a while, but it lacks the true fulfillment of maturity, love, and sacrifice.

The apostle Paul, one of the greatest missionaries the world has ever known, quoted his Master in his farewell address to the elders at Ephesus:

In everything I did, I showed you that by this kind of hard work we must help the weak, remembering the words the Lord Jesus himself said: 'It is more blessed to give than to receive'" (Acts 20:35).

Will we enter into that blessing by giving to others? By taking responsibility for our nations and the destiny of our children's children. We must decide to move from deliverance to freedom, from the desert to Caanan, for freedom is our destiny. *Free-dom*inion is the liberty to dominate the earth and fulfill God's ultimate purpose for all mankind.

"True leaders work for the benefit of others and not for personal gain."

Chapter 6

Are You Really Free?

"Change the leader, change the follower."

Most people have their own definition of freedom that often differs from the next person's idea. Our definition of freedom comes from our learned behavior. We may have gained our view of freedom through books, conversations, or television. Our connotation of freedom may have been passed down through family, cultural, institutional, or religious tradition. No matter how it came to us, we all possess different views on the concept of freedom.

If I say freedom and you think something different from what I mean, then understanding is not present. Understanding takes place when definitions of terms are the same. This is why the Bible says that as believers in the Lord Jesus we are to be of the same mind, which is the mind of Christ. Therefore it is necessary for the sake of clarity to present a working definition and understanding of freedom that will concur with the biblical perspective of freedom.

In order for you to accurately understand what freedom is, you must also know what it is not. First, freedom is not the absence of chains or physical restraints. In fact, freedom is not the absence of restrictions in general. Second, freedom is not given by other people. This element of freedom is more difficult to comprehend than any other. The misconception is that other people possess our freedom. Third, true freedom can never be given to you. Not only can people not bestow freedom upon you, but authentic biblical freedom cannot be given.

When you consider this list of what freedom is not, it poses a problem when evaluating freedom according to our traditional standards. If I confine you to prison and throw away the key, it does not necessarily mean you are not free. Freedom has very little to do with your external environment.

What is freedom? In order to sufficiently define freedom, we must first identify the source of it. If you go to someone to get your freedom, you have just given that person control over your existence.

This has been the single greatest misconception and weakness of my brethren after the flesh who struggle with the civil rights issue. For this reason, like the apostle Paul, I have great sorrow and anguish in my heart because of the continued cultural and spiritual oppression that is imposed upon them by the powers that be.

My heart's desire and prayer for all Third World people is that they be delivered from the demonic belief that the government and other human sources hold the keys to their deliverance.

As the sons and daughters of an enslaved and oppressed people, we once had chains on our hands and feet. Those chains were transferred to our minds and spirits by psychological intimidation and cultural, racist propaganda. Now many have transferred those psychological chains to their children.

When you allow a particular group of men to bestow upon you what they think should be your "civil rights" or freedom, you greatly increase your vulnerability to bondage and exploitation in the future. If you presuppose someone has the power to extend to you *rights*, you have just given that someone the *right* to control you. They are given the authority to extend to you "the right to be civil."

Nobody should ever be given the privilege of ascribing to you worth. If you get your value from someone, they can determine how much you are worth. In fact, the real issue is not "civil rights" but human rights. Human rights are inherent in God's creation of man; civil rights is man's opinion of that human being.

The Truth Will Make You Free

Leaders and ministers, remember this truth: You can only lead people as far as you yourself have gone. Therefore, if I demand from you my rights to be a man, you can determine how much you will give me. Freedom, according to the Word of God, cannot be given. In order to illustrate the validity of this point, we must refer to the constitution (the Bible) of our government (the kingdom of God).

As citizens of the kingdom of God, we must know our constitution and its implications. If we don't, our rights and privileges will be abused and many times withheld.

Contrary to popular belief, the devil is not ultimately responsible for the bondage of believers. Satan is not responsible for our lack of freedom.

My people are destroyed from lack of knowledge (Hosea 4:6).

We remain in bondage because we are ignorant of what has been provided for us through the life and death of our Lord and Savior Jesus Christ.

Jesus discussed how one actualizes the reality of authentic freedom. Let us observe how He dealt so eloquently and simply with this subject. If you understand His definition of freedom, liberty will be instantaneous. Jesus' definition of freedom supersedes all other discourses on the subject. Other than the Bible, no book can make you free. No earthly government can give you self-worth. No man-made authority can make you free, not eternally free. Jesus declared:

> If ye continue in my word, then are ye my disciples indeed; and ye shall know the truth, and the truth shall make you free (John 8:31,32, KJV).

He saw true freedom as a result of understanding the truth about yourself and everyone else as is revealed in the Word of God. In other words, no one can give you the right to be free. Freedom is not something you receive; it is something that happens to you. Free men can never be bound. Freedom is a personal discovery of the truth about yourself from the One Who created you. Thus freedom is not bestowed, but embraced.

True Leadership is Freedom

No man is truly free until every man is free. This is the essence of life and the goal of true leadership. Much of what we call freedom is not freedom at all, but simply permission given by an oppressor to become somebody. This is not freedom. If the source of your liberty is another person or a group, then you are only as free as they allow you to be. This is why the civil rights movements of the world simply resulted in sophisticated mental and economic oppression. Freedom cannot be declared in a speech or legislation, but rather personally discovered by the heart and spirit of each individual.

Freedom cannot be given by another. True leadership sets followers free to discover, develop, and deploy themselves to maximize their full potential and purpose. True freedom is a product of truth, not legislation.

The concept of freedom can be seen in the very word "freedom." A grammatical construction of the words "free" and "dominion," it comes from the concept of having the liberty to dominate. This truth is the very heart of man's purpose from creation and is expressed in the very foundation of God's intention for mankind. God declared, "And let them rule . . . over all the earth" (Genesis 1:26).

This established not only the purpose for man's creation, but also the measure of his fulfillment.

In essence, no man is truly free until he has the liberty to dominate his environment, not other men. This is the heart of true leadership: to inspire men to declare independence from the bondage of other men's opinions and prejudgments, and to tap the unlimited potential within them to creatively dominate the earth, which is his destiny. *Therefore, any leadership that restricts, denies, inhibits, limits, suppresses, oppresses, obstructs, or frustrates this God-given mandate and capacity is not leadership at all, but oppressive manipulation.*

Most of the world's people—in every nation, culture, socioeconomic condition, and political situation—endure lives that are daily drudgery. Even in the highly developed, industrialized states where wealth and affluence are accessible, millions experience depression, despair, anxiety, and emptiness. They realize that possessions, fame, status, and power can never replace a personal sense of purpose and significance. This truth is especially important for those who live in Third World nations. Many undeveloped, and now developing, countries were victims of oppression, subjugation, and colonization.

They were raped of dignity, self-worth, and a sense of well-being. Most do not have access to the material possessions that the industrialized cultures use as the standards of wealth and success. This further compounds the frustration and despair among these people. Many have experienced independence and deliverance, and been given "civil rights," but not true human rights and freedom.

Despite these setbacks, however, those who live in Third World nations must begin to grasp their potential for growth. Only when they see the possibilities that lie within them will they fulfill their destiny to take charge of their future and exercise dominion over the earth, not their fellow man.

*"True freedom is a product
of truth, not legislation."*

Chapter 7

Look Inside Yourself

"Some people are open to change as long as it doesn't cost anything."

The great industrial nation, the United States of America, was conceived in the womb of rebellion. The labor pangs of a civil war delivered her into the incubator of a world torn by disillusionment. After wiping away the afterbirth of her internal struggle, this new nation created one of the greatest republics this world has ever known.

At the turn of the century, with the introduction of the industrial revolution, America began to experience social and economic growth. As in everything, however, progress came at a price. In this instance, the foundation for the economic empire of this great nation was built on the backs of human slave labor.

This resulted in the swift development of the industrial society at the expense of entire ethnic groups: most being products of the West African slave trade. An entire segment of the nation was excluded from the benefits of the industrialized society they helped to create. For many years they were victimized by their lower estate. This discrepancy of social and economic justice, however, haunted the nation and continues to exact a heavy toll on the future of the country.

The Urban Challenge

One of the great phenomena of social, economic, and cultural change in these so-called modern societies—nations where oppression of the masses occurred—is the creation of massive urban centers.

The dynamics involved in this transition are complex and demand attention as they directly affect conditions in the entire nation. Fueled by frustration, disillusionment, fear, hopelessness, and distrust, many antisocial activities find their expression in these urban centers. Many live their entire lives in this deadly environment, guided by a desire to survive.

Attempting to address these problems, federal, state, and local governments have spent billions of dollars trying to rectify the situation. Many of their programs have failed miserably, creating additional problems that further compound the dilemma. Reactionary groups and civil rights movements have attempted to alleviate the pressure by fighting for equal justice and opportunities for all, but even this seems to have only created a false sense of hope in the urban centers of these sick societies.

Is there hope for the millions who call these urban centers home? Can the government change the attitude and environment of these populations? Who has the answers? Where do we look to find them?

"Nothing splendid has ever been achieved except by those who dared believe that something inside of them was superior to circumstances."

These words spoken by a great leader aptly describe the spirit that seems to be rising from the ashes of the inner cities of our nations. We must look inside ourselves for these answers.

Today's Followers Are Tomorrow's Leaders

Today over five billion people live on planet earth. Over half these people live in countries that have been labeled Third World–a term coined by a French economist to describe various groupings of people based on their socioeconomic status. Whether or not this term is valid, it is generally accepted as a description for millions of people.

Third World identifies those who were not allowed to benefit from or participate in the industrial revolution. The majority of these people were not allowed to benefit from the industrial revolution because they were subjugated at the time, being used to fuel the economic base for the revolution. Many of them were reduced to slaves and indentured servants, thus robbing them of their identity, dignity, self-worth, and self-respect.

Despite the changes in conditions and a greater measure of freedom and independence, many of these peoples are still grappling with their identity and their sense of self-worth. Many nations that developed through the industrial revolution have reinforced–by attitude, policies, and legislation–the notion that Third World people lack the potential, skills, intelligence, and sophistication necessary to equal that of industrialized states.

Unfortunately, this is a terrible misconception that has limited many talented people. The potential of all Third World peoples everywhere–in Africa, India, Latin America, the Caribbean and Asia–is limitless and cannot be measured by the opinions of others. You possess the ability to achieve, develop, accomplish, produce, create, and perform anything your mind can conceive. God created you with all the potential you need to fulfill your purpose in this life.

The opinions of others should never determine your self-worth. Your identity is not found in the prejudgments of others, but in the source from which you came: God, your Father and Creator. Jesus came to restore you to your rightful position and to reveal to you the awesome potential that is trapped inside you.

The wealth within the Third World must be realized, harnessed, and maximized by its people. We must be willing to work and commit ourselves to tapping the potential in our land, youth, the arts, sports, and music. Our governments must believe that they have the ability to improve on systems and forms institutionalized by the industrialized states.

The Church in the Third World must begin to take responsibility for its own people and realize its potential to write its own songs and books and to develop an indigenous resource management, financial autonomy, and accountability.

We must not inhibit our potential to chart a new course for the future by being preoccupied with the past. We must deposit the wealth of our potential in this generation so the next generation can build their future on our faithfulness to become everything we can possibly be. Just as there is a forest in every seed, there is a new world within your world. Whatever God calls for, He provides for.

Sharpen Your Skills

Historically, Third World peoples have always been hard-working, dedicated, zealous, and highly sensitive. Many of them are products of oppression that has instilled in them timidity, lack of self-confidence, and a spirit of dependency. They often fail to realize the capacity of leadership potential within them. In most of these Third World countries, the system and process of colonization carried with it the dehumanizing element of fostering dependency and robbing individuals of their creative development. This debilitating system also provided its subjects with basic training for service but not for productivity.

In essence, they were taught how to grow sugar cane but not how to make sugar; they were taught how to grow cotton but not how to make cloth. This perpetuated dependency. Even after they were liberated, or "emancipated," they were left with raw materials but no ability to transform them into end products.

Because they were left with the zeal of freedom but not the skill for development, many Third World nations still experience tremendous hardship and turmoil. The industrialized states that once colonized them have maintained a sense of control and superiority that manifests itself in a form of *economic colonialism instead of political colonialism*.

Third World nations still look to the industrially developed states for their measure of standard, quality, and excellence. This breeds a sense of disrespect and suspicion for their own products and a denial of the tremendous potential that lies dormant in these people everywhere.

This denial of potential was also transferred to the church world through missions efforts. Many churches in Third World countries are products of foreign-based missions and in most cases were dependent on a mother church organization. This dependency led to the problem of leaving many of these ministries without well-trained, confident, and competent leaders.

Even though many of these church organizations have qualified and capable indigenous leaders, there is still the notion that the presence of a foreign element is necessary to maintain excellence and quality. A fresh wind of responsibility is blowing through these Third World countries, however, stirring a sense of destiny and purpose in the hearts of these people everywhere. This awakening of the spirit of responsibility is being felt in all arenas: political, social, civic, and spiritual.

Third World people must look for the inner strength and potential lying deep within them. With a renewed commitment to the Creator, Jesus Christ, they must prepare themselves to refine their skills.

> If the ax is dull and its edge unsharpened, more strength is needed but skill will bring success (Ecclesiastes 10:10).

Every man, woman, boy, and girl in every nation and every race must realize the capacity for greatness that lies dormant within them. As we recognize our potential to do mighty things and take steps of faith in that direction, God will bring tremendous change to our world.

There is a season of change gaining momentum throughout the world and among "third world" people everywhere, including those trapped within the concrete jungles of the industrial state. However, seasons of change demand a response and adjustment. Now let us explore this season of change and how we can all effectively respond to it for the benefit of succeeding generations.

"People tend to become what the most important people in their lives think they will become."

Chapter 8

Salvaging the Season

*"Ignoring the season of
change will forfeit destiny."*

The story of the Swiss Watch Company teaches us the importance of understanding and responding effectively to change. For more than a century the undisputed world leader in the industry was the Swiss Watch Company. In fact, the word "watch" became synonymous with Switzerland. Their success as the most efficient watchmakers in the world was unchallenged. Everyone wanted a Swiss watch.

At the height of its reign as the king of the timepiece world, the Swiss Watch Company controlled more than 80 percent of the market. During this time, one of its young researchers, along with a number of his colleagues, invented a new, more accurate, and entirely electronic watch. The excited, youthful inventor was invited to introduce his latest brain-child at a specially called board meeting of the company. He had hoped to set the Swiss Watch Company on a course of remaining the leader in the watch sales market for the future.

As the new product was introduced, the members of the board listened with interest and carefully assessed the change from a motorized to an electronic based product. After careful review, the company decided the invention was interesting and held promise, but they refused to make it a priority. Why? They were satisfied with their century-long success in the world sales market. Their comfortable position in the business contributed to their failure to patent it.

A year later, the Swiss Watch Company displayed the new invention along with its other products at the Annual Watch Congress, and representatives of two companies noticed it. These two companies soon developed a similar prototype based on the principle of electronic operations, and it revolutionized the watch industry worldwide.

The rest of the story is history. The Swiss Watch Company never recovered from this shift in watchmaking. Today the competition is shared among a myriad of innovative companies that struggle to stay in the game. Ten years later, the Swiss Watch Company had less than ten percent of the world watch market profits. This devastating loss forced the company to terminate fifty thousand of its sixty-five thousand employees. They plummeted from the pinnacle to the pits in ten years.

Why did their watches experience a dramatic drop in popularity? The electric watch signaled a new season, a glimpse into the future, but their century of success blinded them to the impending, inevitable reality of change.

The Swiss Watch Company thought their manufacturing method was the only way to make a watch. They assumed their past success guaranteed future profits. They ignored the prospect of constant change. *Their old methods kept them from embracing and benefiting from new ones.*

The story of the Swiss Watch Company is a lesson for every leader today, especially those responsible for the spread and establishment of the kingdom of God in this generation. What is that lesson? *He who fails to expect, plan for, embrace, and adapt to change in the future will regret his past. Ignoring the season of change will cause him to forfeit his destiny.*

The greatest enemy of man is not sin nor Satan but ignorance. What you do not know will destroy you. What is worse is not knowing that you do not know. Many great possibilities were lost to the world because of ignorance. Wise King Solomon wrote:

> Wisdom is supreme; therefore get wisdom. Though it cost all you have, get understanding (Proverbs 4:7).

Understanding is the comprehension of knowledge; wisdom is the application of that knowledge.

In this critical time of transition, change, and shifting seasons, we must understand the times. Scripture says the sons of Issachar were men "who understood the times and knew what Israel should do" (1 Chronicles 12:32). Understanding enables us to know what to do. *If we want to make right decisions and initiate effective action, then we must understand the seasons.* Godly wisdom will allow us to manage the changing times with precision.

> There is a time for everything, and a season for every activity under heaven (Ecclesiastes 3:1).

Natural rhythms exist all around us. God created seasons in nature, in our bodies, and in the weather. The cycles of the planets and the stars also support this principle. Studying the natural will help us to better understand the spiritual.

How can we successfully navigate this turbulent period of transition? We must understand five aspects of times and seasons to appreciate their impact on our lives.

Inherent in seasons are the concepts of:

Change: The very nature of seasons implies change and guarantees a natural inevitability.

Transition: Season denotes the transition of time. It presupposes a point of convergence where two seasons meet.

Difference: Seasons intimate the replacement of one environment or condition with another different from itself.

Temporary conditions: Seasons indicate the nonpermanent nature of conditions in time and assure us that nothing remains the same. In fact, only change is permanent.

Time period: Seasons suggest that present conditions are subject to time and exist within the parameters of a predetermined time-span. Time will bring change.

Understanding the Seasons

The present transitions at this juncture of history are obvious. Anyone who wishes to see it will know change is taking place right now. Let's look at some of the changes that will affect each of us.

1. *Generational Transition:* Many leaders, fathers, and founders of significant organizations, institutions, religious ministries, and governmental bodies are entering the twilight of their lives. Their departure permits the emergence and ascension of new, youthful leadership from a different generation.

2. *Political Transition:* The international balance of power has shifted from the one known by the previous generation. The Cold War has ended. The United States is no longer the lone star police of global affairs. The emergence of a multiplicity of small and large states to important positions in the global equation demands attention. The opening of China—the most populous nation in the world—and the rise of Third World economies, including the nations of South America, Central America, and Africa, create a more complex marketing environment in international affairs.

National and international terrorism has the potential to render vulnerable the economies and social stability of nations. The increased role of the United Nations in international disputes and social concerns is also a part of this complex political new world we are entering.

3. *Religious Transition:* The religious climate is changing around the world. Nations long thought to be Christian strongholds have seen the rise of Islam. The expansion of other eastern mystic religions, including Hinduism, Buddhism, and others, is also a component in this new equation.

Christianity is also undergoing significant changes that demand urgent assessment and understanding. First, the rise of significant and effective national ministers in many Third World countries is undeniable. These same areas were traditionally mission fields for the churches in industrialized nations. This change demands a new approach to international missions strategy and makes obsolete many of the traditional modes of missions.

The Church in industrial countries, which has insinuated the inability of indigenous leaders to take responsibility for their own nation, needs to assume a new attitude and position with regard to how they relate to the church in Third World environments.

4. *Spiritual Transition:* This may seem paradoxical to separate this change from the religious, but it's necessary to understand that the spiritual change presently taking place is one of divine transfer. Many Third World countries are

experiencing an uprising of spiritual leadership and effective ministry development. This indicates that the future spiritual revival will be focused on developing nations.

The transition spiritually seems to be from north to south, from old to young, from the known to the unknown, from the expected to the unexpected. The hand of the Lord is definitely moving among nations, producing a spiritual sense of nationalism–a spirit of responsibility for national salvation. A core of new leadership is emerging from the shadows.

5. *Economic Transition:* The global economic trend is in a state of change, producing drastic repercussions. We see a shift from national to global market economies, from north to south, from west to east, and from local to national. The spirit of interdependence in economies is now a reality. The isolationist policies of post World War II are inappropriate for our global village. Everyone is affected by everyone.

The growth of the developing nations produces stronger economic environments, which result in stronger money markets. This also provides more resources for ministry development in nations once considered poor and helpless. These changes will affect us all. Economic change also includes the improved management of resources in countries where the skills of effective management were lacking.

6. *Social Transition:* In recent years the social infrastructure of many nations has been transformed by increased access to formal education, the explosion of the information age, the access to formal and informal long-distance education programs, and the expansion of travel. These factors have produced more internationally educated citizens. In fact, the average individual of today's world is much more sophisticated than those of fifty years ago. Therefore any attempt to evangelize or influence people must consider the improved education factor.

7. *Cultural Transition:* This is a major element of change in our fast shrinking world. The ease of global transportation has produced a very mobile world population, which has diluted the level of distinction and isolation of cultures among the nations of the earth.

Cultures that were once foreign to each other are now neighbors. In some cases, one culture has overtaken another. This change has a direct bearing on one's ability to communicate, understand, and effectively influence cultures different from his own. This change must not be ignored. He who refuses to venture, explore, and learn other cultures will be culturally illiterate in this 21st century. To be effective in the age of the new world, one must be an *international citizen*. The new paradigm for education must also reflect this changing environment.

A Prototype of Our Future

The title of a cover story in *USA Today* (September 1997) read, "Educators Challenged by Diversity's Demand." The article reported on the drastic change being experienced by the United States through the influx of immigrants from a multitude of nations, bringing with them their culture, languages, and unique heritage. The article reported: "Students from the Fairfax County Public Schools come from 182 countries and speak more than 100 languages. Fairfax County is one of five school districts in the United States in which more than 100 languages are spoken, according to the U. S. Department of Education. One is in New York. The others are all in Washington, D.C. and its suburbs."

Referring specifically to Annandale High School in the town of Annandale, Virginia, the reports stated, "As extreme as it is today, Annandale High is a harbinger of America's not-so-distant future, when half of all public school students will be minorities, and no group will dominate the ethnic landscape. The diversity of these schools is creating pressure for educators."

The report continues: "By the year 2025, fifty percent of all public school students in America will be minority students. That's going to challenge the whole definition of minority and nonminority. *This is going to mean youngsters are going to have to respect different cultures, ethnicities, and races.*"

This prophetic report then made a startling statement: "Just over a decade ago Annandale High was more than 90 percent white but today of its roughly 2,000 students, 43 percent go home to families that speak a language other than English."

What does this mean to leaders of the 21st century? It demands a new approach to everything. The exclusive nature of historical ethnic isolation is over. *It means that all leadership training for the future must prepare individuals for a multicultural experience. The mandate of the Church from the beginning was global and multicultural in scope. It requires a multinational, inclusive, trans-generational, interracial ministry that transcends social strategy.* If the Christian leader or layman will be effective in this new 21st century, then he must embrace change and adapt to its demands. He must be willing to change old, ineffective methods, modes, and attitudes.

Embracing the Season

One word that has become a common part of our everyday language in recent years is paradigm. *What is a paradigm?* It's a model or pattern, or a way of thinking and acting. When changes occur in models, patterns, or ways of thinking, they are called paradigm shifts. Such shifts occur during a generational transfer, when old styles become inadequate as a result of new demands, and when old methods develop into new problems. The present providential change in seasons demands a paradigm shift in all areas of ministry and leadership. Those who fail to understand the times and seasons will find themselves irrelevant in reaching the world.

This seasonal change includes a divine shift in leadership, location, focus, emphasis, priorities, and methods. It is, therefore, imperative that we look at how to prepare for the change, how to respond to the change, how to maximize the change, and what to do to change ourselves in order to fulfill God's purpose in this generation.

The Leadership Change

A paradigm shift is currently taking place in every arena. Across the globe, leaders are sensing an urgency to respond to changes they know they must embrace. The old style and methods of leadership has lost its effectiveness and must yield to the new equation of 21st century leadership.

This area of change is critical because the impact of leaders on organizations, institutions, and ministries is crucial. The focus on the emerging Third World leadership in both the social, political, and religious fields is undeniable. Whether you live in the modern industrial society or in the developing Third World, you must carefully consider how this change affects your life and leadership.

For more than five hundred years, the system of colonization by European empires of Africa, the Caribbean, the West Indies, the Far East, South America, and other territories of the western world—and the subsequent displacement of peoples through the slave trade—have served as the foundation of the present western societies that exist today. But we must remember the scriptural principle, "to everything there is a season." Nothing lasts forever.

During this period, the expansion of the Christian Church followed the colonization routes. Christian missionaries from the industrial nations felt an obligation to Christianize the new lands and the peoples over which they exercised dominion. These efforts produced significant missions establishments that developed a system of mother-church-dependent national ministries supported by external leadership and resources.

It is understandable that this phase of missions was perhaps necessary but also seasonal. After five hundred years of missions efforts in these so-called Third World countries, many of them have gained political independence and are now on a course to determining their own national destiny. This major seasonal change has also given way to a new sense of national confidence in the Church in these nations.

If you as a parent observed that your children never grew up but remained dependent upon you all their lives, your concerns and questions about your effectiveness as a parent would be reasonable. Independence and interdependence are signs of growth and maturity. This is the present season. The children have grown, and the parents must accept and adjust to the change.

This is very significant because it means that the leadership in these emerging nations must prepare for the responsibility of guiding and disciplining their nations.

Responding to the Season

Change affects everyone. Even if you refuse to change, change will change you. Change will happen to you, with you, around you, and without you. This is the nature of seasons. If we are to respond effectively to the changing season, then we must not ignore the truth about the future. It holds one of two destinies for you: change or failure. *You have the power to determine the quality and effectiveness of your future by your response to change.*

This new season of change will be difficult for many. Why? Because nothing is more secure than the familiar. In fact, the most uncomfortable word in the English language is change. Being creatures of habit, we dread the thought of change. Change is a principle of life, however, so we must learn to live with it. It is said that change occurs only when the pain of remaining the same exceeds the pain of change. You must respond. God knows His agenda for the 21st century, and He is getting us ready for it.

If we are to effectively manage our transition to the next century, we must understand the six characteristics of seasons.

1. *Seasons are natural.* The change of seasons in the church and the world is a natural fulfillment of God's purpose, and His ways are perfect. Because these changes are natural, the effects are first felt in the heart. For example, the shift in focus to the Third World countries and oppressed peoples occurred all over the world at the same time. The Spirit of God began to

prepare them for a more responsible role in leadership in the 21st century. I have traveled to over fifty nations and discovered the same phenomenon—a sudden sense of confidence, destiny, responsibility, and leadership in the hearts of thousands of unsung leaders.

Concurrently, I have also discovered a change in the hearts of thousands of leaders in the industrial states who have held the reins of leadership, influence, and authority for decades. Many have actually admitted this reality and announced this change publicly.

2. *Seasons cannot be stopped.* This characteristic is vital to our response to seasons. Nothing can stop a season. The power that controls a season is beyond our comprehension and defies our logic. Despite the fact that we posses a free will, it is limited to the sovereign purposes of God.

Many are the plans in a man's heart, but it is the Lord's purpose that prevails (Proverbs 19:21).

None of our crying, praying, binding, loosing, anger, or plans can stop winter. Neither can they stop the season of God's purpose in this generation. The change is inevitable. It has arrived in the fullness of time. The beginning and ending of a season are not determined by man but by God's sovereign agenda.

The Lord Almighty has purposed, and who can thwart him? (Isaiah 14:27).

3. *Seasons cannot be resisted.* If a man stood dressed in his swimming trunks, shaking his fist at an impending snowstorm and refusing to accept the approach of winter, you would consider him a fool. The same is true of resisting God's purpose in raising up the formerly opposed, rejected, and ignored to places of leadership, influence, and effective ministry. If anyone resists or fights this season, it will destroy him even as winter freezes the defiant swimmer to death.

4. *Seasons are no respecter of persons.* The defiant swimmer just mentioned may be the mayor of a city, the president of a nation, a lawyer, a king, or a great evangelist, prophet, pastor, or apostle. He would still be frozen to death. Why? Because seasons do not regard rank. No matter who you are, the changing season does not care about your title, accomplishments, or past positions. You must submit to what God is doing. *Seasons demand submission.*

5. *Seasons come without permission.* Some believe they can determine, dictate, and manipulate God's sovereign will. Many have declared what would or would not happen. Others, motivated by a desire to protect their convictions and pre-

serve their present positions, have predicted revivals and pronounced movements that are contrary to what is happening around the world. But we must understand that seasons are controlled by God. They do not require the permission of a group of distinguished, influential leaders to be initiated. We must remember we are only players in a brief portion of history. As such, we should be committed to fulfilling our assignment in our fading generation. *The arrival or demise of a season does not need our blessing; it contains its own.*

6. *Seasons bring change you cannot control.* Have you ever stood in the heat of summer or in the frigid air of winter? What could you do? Nothing, of course. We are helpless to change the season. This is also true of the seasons of unfolding destiny. No matter what our personal desires, wishes, or attitudes may be, they cannot control a season.

In this transition to the 21st century, some have tried to direct or control the providential move of God. Others have tried to take credit and label the change as a personal accomplishment. But the Creator will not have it. This new season will not be controlled. It won't be the trophy of any group, individual, or organization.

A Word to the Victims of Change

Each of us must determine how we will respond to the changing season. No matter who we are or what our position, we are all victims of the seasons. The new season is upon us, and change will come whether we want it or not. The question is, how do we respond?

We are standing in a crucial time in history. Our generation is in the balance. A dramatic paradigm shift is in progress, and you are a part of it. You are entrusted by God to be stewards of this great historic moment and to see its establishment in the earth. This transition will be difficult for those who refuse to accept the season. New leaders will have to understand that many old leaders will not surrender. Those holding onto old ideas are often intimidated by those proposing new ideas. What will you do with change?

There are two victims of providential seasons: those to whom change is happening and those through whom change is happening. For instance, the present leadership order is giving way to a new one. The emerging Third World leadership and the decreasing influence of the former power base demand a major adjustment in every way. Let's look at these changes and how each of us should respond.

Is Change Happening to You?

When change occurs, many people initially experience confusion, fear, desperation, and anger. If we are to benefit from change, however, we must understand our role in the process of change. What can you do if you're being pulled by the tide of transition?

1. *Do not pretend that change is not happening.* When change threatens our comfort and security, we're tempted to retreat into a world of denial. We must seek to understand change, accept its reality, and commit to fulfilling the new role it demands from us.

2. *Do not be angry at change.* Nothing is as immobilizing as an angry spirit. It produces irrational behavior and self-destructive decisions. *The lure of the past can make the prospect of a new future unsettling,* causing one to attack rather than embrace the potential of promise. Be honest with life and oneself. Understand the value of your past and present role. Each of us is important to God's great program of purpose. The religious zealots of Jesus' day reacted in this way and missed the hour of their visitation.

3. *Do not defy change.* In an attempt to protect our fragile sense of importance, security, and significance, we often retreat into a world of our own making rather than accept the truth of life.

We must adapt to change and participate in the transition process instead of fighting the hand of God.

After the resurrection of Christ, the apostles preached boldly. An angry crowd wanted to put them to death. Gamaliel, a Pharisee and a teacher of the law, warned the religious community, "If it is from God, you will not be able to stop these men; you will only find yourselves fighting against God" (Acts 5:39).

Show the maturity that is characteristic of true leaders. You can become a part of the process of God that always works for our good. Christians who are "called according to His purpose" can have this confidence in any situation, no matter how unsettling.

4. *Do not be idle to change.* We can be tempted to withdraw from active participation in the purposes of God as a way of expressing dissatisfaction with His will. The deadly attitude is one that says, "If I am not in charge and in control, then I will not get involved." This immature, fatalistic mentality reduces one to becoming a part of the problem rather than a component of provision in God's plan.

It is essential that we all find our place in God's program and fulfill our purpose no matter what the new role may be.

Can you imagine the major adjustment that Mary and Joseph made to recede into the background as their Son, Jesus, took center stage in the drama of redemption? He whom they once called son would later have to be called Lord. They were not idle. They knew their roles and played them fully. As a result of their faithfulness, they are forever etched in the pages of history as change agents.

Is Change Happening Through You?

Change is inevitable and will happen with or without our permission. When change is initiated through us, what should be our role? For those who are participants in the transition, I suggest the following:

1. *Do not be ignorant of change.* Many people are unaware of the nature of the change they are experiencing. They lack knowledge of God's season for their lives and aren't prepared to participate in their season. Study the times, expand your knowledge, and be open to the Holy Spirit who will reveal the times and the seasons.

2. *Do not be unprepared for change.* God always demands preparation for impending change. This is because He is omniscient. He knows the future. If we are to harness the coming season

and fully participate in the purposes of God, we must prepare for the role we are required to play. For instance, the emerging leaders of Third World nations must urgently address the quality of leadership skills and attitudes of responsibility if they don't want to forfeit their season in God's agenda.

We must understand that, like the children of Israel in Moses' season of deliverance, being chosen does not prepare you for the choice. *You must prepare yourself.* Remember that the children of Israel did not enter the promised land. They weren't prepared to leave the mentality of Egypt.

Improve your skills. Pursue the necessary study and training for your role in the next season. *Seasons do not guarantee success. They simply guarantee change.*

3. *Do not boast in your season.* The Israelites' journey from Egypt to Canaan demonstrates the danger of becoming so preoccupied with your season that you forget the purpose for your season.

They interpreted their being chosen by God to mean that they were superior to those for whom they were chosen to serve. God chose them as a nation unto Himself so they could show the heathen and other pagan nations the true God. The goal was to restore them to worship and relationship with the true and only God.

We must not consider our season as an opportunity for revenge, spite, or superiority. Just as the stewards of the past season failed in many ways to fulfill their purpose, we too could be replaced by the next generation. Let humility, understanding, and sensitivity be trademarks of the new leadership.

4. *Do not be afraid of the season.* It is natural for anxiety, uncertainty, and fear to accompany any venture into unknown territory. As the seasons come upon us, this common experience touches both those to whom change is happening and those through whom change takes place.

Remember that whatever God calls for, He provides for. God gave you potential, ability, gifts, and talents to manage the responsibilities of your season. You are able to change. You are capable of leadership in this generation. Do not doubt your call. Don't shrink from responsibility. Rise to the task, knowing that you were designed for this moment and destined to be a leader in your time. Your time has come. You will be able to take charge. Let change transform your fear into faith. March to the drumbeat of your season. Future generations depend on you. It's your turn.

I trust you gained new insight into your destiny as you read these pages. Perhaps you are one to whom change is happening. You may be the object of the next season. Whatever your role, you are now responsible for your participation in your generation. The season of change is upon you, and you must respond. What you decide will be a testimony to your children and the generations to come.

I pray that you accept the reality of change, adapt to its demands, commit to your role, and prepare for the next season that will follow yours, always mindful that your season is not forever. Make history by preparing for it. Be someone who makes things happen!

"The season of change is upon you."

OTHER BOOKS BY DR. MYLES MUNROE

Becoming A Leader (workbook also available)
Myles Munroe on Leadership
How to Transform Your Ideas into Reality
Single, Married, Separated and Life After Divorce
Understanding Your Potential (workbook also available)
Releasing Your Potential
Maximizing Your Potential
The Pursuit of Purpose
Sex and Relationships
Sex 101

OTHER BOOKS FROM PNEUMA LIFE PUBLISHING

Becoming A Leader
by Dr. Myles Munroe

Many consider leadership to be no more than staying ahead of the pack, but that is a far cry from what leadership is. Leadership is deploying others to become as good as or better than you are. within each of us lies the potential to be an effective leader. *Becoming A Leader* uncovers the secrets of dynamic leadership that will show you how to be a leader in your family, school, community, church and job. No matter where you are or what you do in life this book can help you to inevitably become a leader. Remember: it is never too late to become a leader. As in every tree there is a forest, so in every follower there is a leader. (Workbook also available.)

Myles Munroe on Leadership
Inspirational Quotes for the Frontline Leader

Your road to success is paved by the successes and failures of others who have gone before you. Along the way, other great leaders have paused to encourage you by sharing their inspiration, guiding vision, and passion for accomplishment. In this book, Myles Munroe will give you a whole new perspective on what it means to become an effective leader. This book is a gallery of superb ideas on leadership and how it relates to influence, self-mastery, determination, courage, criticism and countless other eye-opening ideas.

Myles Munroe On Leadership will reveal to you infinite possibilities for reaching your full leadership potential. Rediscover your hidden talents for leadership at the highest level possible. Here are the answers you have always wanted. Myles Munroe takes the mystery out of leadership by unlocking the secrets of over 150 enlightening new insights

The Minister's Topical Bible
Contributor - Dr. Myles Munroe
The Minister's Topical Bible covers every aspect of the ministry providing quick and easy access to Scriptures in a variety of ministry related topics. This handy reference tool can be effectively used in leadership training, counseling, teaching, sermon preparation, and personal study.

The African Cultural Heritage Topical Bible
Contributor - Dr. Myles Munroe
The African Cultural Heritage Topical Bible is a quick and convenient reference Bible. It has been designed for use in personal devotions as well as group Bible studies. It's the newest and most complete reference Bible designed to reveal the Black presence in the Bible and highlight the contributions and exploits of Blacks from the past to present. It's a great tool for students, clergy, teachers — practically anyone seeking to learn more about the Black presence in Scripture, but didn't know where to start.
The African Cultural Heritage Topical Bible contains:
• Over 3**95** easy to find **topics**
• **3,840 verses** that are systematically organized
• A comprehensive listing of Black Inventions
• Over **150 pages** of Christian Afrocentric articles on Blacks in the Bible, Contributions of Africa, African Foundations of Christianity, Culture, Identity, Leadership, and Racial Reconciliation written by **Myles Munroe**, Wayne Perryman, Dr. Leonard Lovett, Dr. Trevor L. Grizzle, James Giles, and Mensa Otabil.

The Church
by Turnel Nelson
Discover God's true intent and purpose for His Church in this powerful release by Pastor Turnel Nelson. This book speaks to the individual with an exciting freshness and urgency to become the true Bride of Christ.

Making the Most of Your Teenage Years
by David Burrows
Discover who you really are – and how to plan for the three phases of your life. You can develop your skill, achieve your dreams, and still have fun.

Strategies for Saving the Next Generation
by David Burrows
This book will teach you how to start and effectively operate a vibrant youth ministry. Dave Burrows offers the reader vital information that will produce results if carefully considered and adapted.

Mobilizing Human Resources
by Richard Pinder
Pastor Pinder gives an in-depth look at how to organize, motivate and deploy members of the body of Christ in a manner that produces maximum effect for your ministry.

Wife 101
Everything Your Husband Wished You Already Knew
Wife 101 gives you two hundred incredible ways to create a more exciting and meaningful relationship. You will gain a new sense of confidence by understanding the things your husband needs from you to function in harmony with you. You will understand how to communicate with the language of his heart. **Wife 101** will give you endless streams of new insights about your marriage from your husband's perspective.

Husband 101
Everything Your Wife Wished You Already Knew
Husband 101 will give your marriage the "booster shot" you've been looking for. **Husband 101** will show you how to recapture the flame of your wife's passion for you again and again. **Husband 101** is a step-by-step mini-course in how to begin an engaging new love affair with your wife.

Available at your local bookstore

Pneuma Life Publishing
4451 Parliament Place
Lanham, MD 20706
(800) 727-3218
(301) 577-4052

Dr. Myles Munroe
Diplomat Center
P.O. Box N9583
Nassau, Bahamas
(242) 341-6444